MAL FAMILIES

Chimpanzees

About this book

Why do many animals gather in family and larger groups? Why do bees dance and wolves howl? How do lions hunt together and zebras defend against them? These and hundreds of other fascinating animal behavior questions are answered in this new set of books about animal life. The books provide fascinating insights into the activities and bodies of all sorts of animals, from meerkat troop signals to honeybee nectar searches, and from ostrich feet to elephant trunks. In each book there are detailed examples of how animals behave, and how they relate to each other. Each book also has lots of photos and specially drawn illustrations. After you have read the book, if you are interested in finding out more about a particular animal, look at the Further Reading section on page 30. It has books and websites to check out. A Glossary on page 31 explains words that you may not be familiar with, and the Index on page 32 tells you where in the book to find a particular animal, behavior, or place.

Published 2001 by Grolier Educational
Sherman Turnpike
Danbury, Connecticut 06816

© 2001 Brown Partworks Limited.

Library of Congress Cataloging-in-Publication Data
Animal Families
p.cm.
Contents: v. 1. Ants/John Woodward — v. 2. Bats/John Jackson — v. 3. Bison/John Woodward — v. 4. Chimpanzees/John Woodward — v. 5. Dolphins/Bridget Giles — v. 6. Elephants/Daniel Gilpin — v. 7. Honeybees/John Woodward — v. 8. Kangaroos/Jen Green — v. 9. Lions/John Woodward — v. 10. Meerkats/Tom Jackson — v. 11. Ostriches/Jen Green — v. 12. Penguins/Daniel Gilpin — v. 13. Prairie Dogs/Jen Green — v. 14. Weaverbirds/Tim Harris — v. 15. Wolves/Jen Green — v. 16. Zebras/Bridget Giles.
ISBN 0-7172-9585-0 (set: alk. paper)
ISBN 0-7172-9588-5 (v. 4: alk. paper)
1. Animal behavior—Juvenile literature. [1. Animals—Habits and behavior.]
I. Grolier Educational Corporation.
QL751.5.A565 2001
591.5-dc21
00-042669

Printed and bound in Singapore.

FOR BROWN PARTWORKS LIMITED
Author: John Woodward
Consultant: Dr. Adrian Seymour
Project editor: Tim Harris
Managing editor: Anne O'Daly
Picture research: Adrian Bentley
Index: Margaret Mitchell

PICTURE CREDITS
Artworks: AntBits Illustration

Bruce Coleman Collection: (Gunter Ziesler) 8, 11, 16–17. *Corbis:* (Henry Diltz) 29 above; (Karl Amman) 9; (Kennan Ward) 10, 12–13. *Image Bank:* (Jeff Hunter) 20; (Joseph van Os) 22. *NHPA:* (Ann & Steve Toon) 15 above; (Christophe Ratier) 7; (Daniel Heuclin) 12; (E. A. Janes) 23; (Martin Harvey) title page, 14, 15 below, 17 below, 28, 29 below; (Steve Robinson) 5 below, 19, 21, 25. *OSF:* (Clive Bromhall) 17 above. *Still Pictures:* (Fritz Polking) 5 above; (John Cancalosi) front cover, 4; (Michel Gunther) contents page, 6, 18, 26, 27.

Series created by Brown Partworks Limited.
Designed by Wilson Design Associates.

Contents

Introduction

There is something very special about chimpanzees. Every one is different, with its own character. It has its own likes and dislikes. It has to learn most of its skills, and it might be good at some and hopeless at others. It might even invent a totally new skill and show it to its friends.

Does all this seem familiar? Of course it does. Chimpanzees are like us. That is hardly surprising because they are our nearest *Wrong* living relatives. Chimps and humans are descended from the same ancestors, who lived in Africa between 5 million and 7 million years ago.

While early humans took to walking upright on the open plains, chimpanzees became adapted for living in the forests. They have longer arms, fingers, and toes for reaching and clinging to branches. Although chimps use their hands to climb through trees and usually walk on all fours, they also use their hands to make and use simple tools. They have complicated social

▶ *A young chimpanzee and its mother. The young usually stay with their mothers until they are at least five years, and sometimes much older.*

4

▲ *Chimpanzees are equally at home on the ground and up in the trees.*

lives, and their own language of signs and sounds. Given the chance, a chimpanzee can even learn ways of communicating with humans.

In this book you will discover how chimp society works, and how chimps spend their days. You will also see what makes them so special—and so like us.

Brainpower

Chimpanzees have big brains compared to their size, and they are very intelligent. Chimpanzees are capable of solving relatively complex practical problems. They learn from their friends, so different communities of chimps deal with the same problems in different ways. This is what makes chimpanzees so unpredictable, and why their behavior is so fascinating.

▶ *Young chimpanzees are able to learn skills by watching the adults in their group. This one is preparing a stick to use as a digging tool.*

Chimpanzee communities

All chimpanzees live in communities of between 15 and 120 individuals. Each community shares an area called its home range. It often overlaps with the ranges of neighboring communities. If food is scarce, the range can be huge, covering up to 150 square miles (400 sq km); but in tropical forests with lots of fruiting trees it usually covers between 4 and 20 square miles (10 to 50 sq km).

The chimps in the community use the home range in different ways. Each adult female has her own special part of the range, which she shares with her young.

The females often meet to feed at fruiting trees and sometimes form special friendships.

Adult males roam all over the home range, often in parties of three to six. They are more

▼ *Chimpanzees can be very affectionate, as this young chimp and its mother are showing.*

Pushing their luck

As young chimps play with each other, they find out what other chimps like and dislike. They soon discover that they can push some chimps farther than others. They challenge each other and start developing their own pecking order, or hierarchy. These are useful lessons for the future.

▼ *A community of chimps will roam around its home range in search of food.*

Jostling for position

Male chimpanzees have a complicated social life. They compete against each other for status and females, but they also form alliances to defend the community and their own position within it. They normally avoid serious arguments, but sometimes rival chimps refuse to back down. They glare at each other; and if neither gives in, they may fight. They grab, kick, and bite; but if they are from the same community, they rarely do any real damage.

sociable than females, but they are always arguing over who's boss. There is a definite pecking order in chimp society, especially among males, and it keeps changing as young chimps get strong enough to show how tough they are. When different parties get together after a few days apart, there is always a noisy reunion as they shout, scream, hug, and threaten each other, all trying to climb just a bit farther up the social ladder.

Social skills

Chimpanzees are very emotional animals, and they show it. When they meet, after a few days apart, there is always a lot of hugging and kissing, as well as challenging and scrapping. They show anger, fear, joy, and devotion, as well as a lot of less obvious emotions and feelings. They are always communicating these things to each other with their bodies, faces, and voices, so they all know what is going on.

Chimpanzee body language is easy to understand. A dominant chimp swaggers around with shoulders hunched and hair bristling, brandishing a broken branch. Meanwhile, a submissive chimp crouches with his back turned, peering fearfully over his shoulder.

▼ *Chimpanzees groom each other to show affection or to patch up quarrels.*

Grooming

When the dust settles after a chimpanzee reunion, they all sit down to groom each other. Grooming is obviously valuable to hairy animals who cannot see some parts of their bodies. Sensitive fingers pick off mud, flaking skin, and parasites such as ticks, helping to keep them healthy. But offering to groom another chimp is also a way of making friends.

Chimps groom each other to patch up quarrels, get something they want, win allies, or just to show their affection. Dominant chimps get groomed a lot, but they return the compliment. It's a very important way of cementing the community together.

Facial expressions

Facial expressions are more difficult to understand, for us at any rate. An angry chimp clenches his mouth firmly, but a fearful chimp often grins, showing his clenched teeth in a way that looks quite fierce. Yet these are just two of a wide range of expressions. They are backed up by 13 different types of call, each with many variations. When used together, they allow chimpanzees to convey all kinds of information to each other.

▲ *These chimpanzees are showing their feelings: from left to right, relaxed, worried, happy, and frightened.*

▶ *Chimpanzees communicate with body language as well as noises. This chimp is demonstrating its frustration.*

Sign language

Since chimps are so expressive, scientists have tried to teach them the sign language used by deaf people. Some chimps have shown quite a talent for this, learning the signs for many words and stringing them together into simple sentences. They may not be able to talk, but they have other ways of speaking.

Finding food

Chimpanzees are like us: they'll eat almost anything, provided they can digest it. They avoid grass and tough leaves because, like us, they can't get enough nutrients from them: it would be like eating cardboard. They need richer food, and their favorite is ripe fruit. Fruit contains a lot of sugar and vitamins but very little protein, so to get it chimps eat young, tender leaves. They also enjoy flowers, nuts, a little meat, and insects such as ants, caterpillars, and termites.

They eat fruit for about four hours a day, usually in the morning. Rain forest trees come into fruit at different times throughout the year. These fruiting trees are scattered all over the home range, so the community splits up into feeding parties that target particular trees. Chimps have an amazing ability to remember when each tree bears fruit; and when they set off each morning, they usually know exactly where they are going.

When they find a good tree, they celebrate by making a great deal of noise. The commotion

◄ *Chimpanzees sometimes kill and eat other animals. This one is eating a baboon, which may have been killed by a hunting party.*

Hunting parties

Chimpanzees are not just peaceful fruit eaters. They can be killers too. Insects are their main prey, but they often pounce on larger animals. Usually they surprise small monkeys, pigs, and antelopes in places where the prey cannot easily escape; but some chimps—usually males—organize full-scale hunts.

Colobus monkeys are favorite targets. A group of males may spot a colobus and carefully climb into position to block its escape routes. Then one or two chimps drive the monkey into an ambush. They rip it apart with shrieks of triumph and eat it on the spot.

▲ *Groups of chimpanzees search the forest for trees bearing ripe fruit. When they find one, they hoot in triumph, attracting others to join the feast.*

often draws other chimps to share the feast, and a big, heavily laden tree may attract 20 or more. They pluck the fruit with their hands; and unless they are really hungry, they often discard any seeds or tough skins. By midday they are ready for a few hours' rest. They feed again in the afternoon, usually on leaves, then look for a safe tree where they can settle for the night.

The mating game

Sex plays a big part in chimpanzee life. All the adults in a community seem to mate with each other, and the young ones soon start copying them. It all looks very casual and disorganized, but it isn't.

A female chimp knows she can win useful friends by mating with them; so when she comes into breeding condition every month, she starts flirting with high-ranking males. The males usually make the first move, but the female is happy to oblige. She may mate with several males a day for a week or so, but at this stage she cannot become pregnant. As soon as she is able to get pregnant, things start to get really serious.

A male can tell when a female is in breeding condition because her rump swells up like a pink cushion. When it reaches maximum size, it means she is ready to mate, and the males suddenly become very jealous of each other. Usually one dominant male tries to keep her to himself by closely following her, grooming her, and driving away rival males.

Most baby chimps are the result of these pairings, although the males can never be really sure which are their own—sometimes a rival chimp mates with the female when the dominant male isn't around.

▲ *A chimp family group: adult male, mother, and baby.*

◀ *The swollen pink rump of this female shows that she is in breeding condition.*

Sneaky moves

Although dominant male chimps manage to father most of the children in the community, they don't have it all their own way. Lower-ranking males may try to lure females away from them.

One of these hopefuls may sit near a couple, gazing at the female. When they all move off to find food, he makes a point of going in a different direction, watching to see if she is following. If she likes him, they may slip away into the forest together. It all has to be done very carefully, though, because if her original partner realizes what is going on, there is big trouble.

Long childhood

A mother chimpanzee is pregnant for seven or eight months, and she usually has just one baby at a time. The newborn chimp is quite helpless, and his mother has to hold the baby against her as she moves around. Eventually he gets a grip, though, and is able to hang on by himself.

As she feeds her baby on her milk, the mother tries to stay close to other mothers or friendly males for protection. Males from other chimp communities sometimes attack their neighbors, and babies are often the first to suffer. At about six months the young chimp starts riding on his mother's back for a better view of the world.

About this time he begins experimenting with solid foods. His mother has to show him what he can and cannot eat, since he has no idea. By the age of about four he is weaned off milk

▼ *Young chimps are almost always playing. This group is having a rest after some energetic games.*

Early learning

Young chimpanzees learn almost everything they know by watching the adults in their community. They copy the way they make their nests, find food, and use tools. And if a young chimp gets it wrong, his or her mother is likely to demonstrate the right way.

Deliberate teaching is very rare among animals, but chimpanzees do it. On one occasion a mother chimp was watching her daughter trying to crack nuts using a stone. Each time she failed. After 10 minutes the mother moved over to her daughter, who gave her the stone and watched while the adult carefully showed her student the right way to do it.

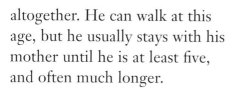

▲ Young chimpanzees learn by watching their elders.

altogether. He can walk at this age, but he usually stays with his mother until he is at least five, and often much longer.

Baby chimps play constantly. They chase each other around trees, run, and climb. This makes them fit and agile, and they discover how to get along with each other. They learn to give and take, and how to interpret the expressions and sounds made by their elders. It is all useful experience.

▶ Mothers carry around their babies until they are about six months old.

Male gangs

By the age of five or six a young male chimp is learning to look after himself. He makes his own sleeping nest and finds most of his own food.

▼ *If a lone male chimpanzee wanders into a neighboring territory, he may have to run away quickly from its resident chimps.*

He no longer depends on his mother for everything, and he starts showing an interest in male society. He challenges other young males to trials of strength and starts trailing around after the big adult males. At the age of eight or nine he may be adopted by one adult as an apprentice, and he starts learning what being a male chimp is all about.

Chimpanzee society is based on groups of related males—fathers, brothers, and cousins—who defend their home range

▲ *The large male at the center is chasing away the other chimps.*

Border patrol

Most border clashes between neighboring males are accidental, and they are often settled by shows of strength and loud hooting. But every few days parties of males go on deliberate border patrols, looking for trouble. They creep silently through the forest, watching and listening. If they see their neighbors, they may spy on them for a while, then slip away. They may show themselves and put on a noisy display. Or they may attack.

These raids are often ruthless attempts to steal territory and capture females. If the raiders run into a lone male, they attack him, some pinning him down while the others kick and bite. Many are killed. In western Tanzania whole communities of males have been wiped out by their neighbors.

against males from neighboring communities. Although they squabble over status, they form close friendships and work easily as a team. Since they stay on their home range for life, they know every tree and stream, and exactly where the boundaries lie. They spend a lot of time near these boundaries, so it is not long before a young male gets to see some serious action.

► *This is the dominant male of a community of 45 chimps, also known as the alpha male.*

Migrant females

A young female chimpanzee stays with her mother for slightly longer than her brothers. When she is about 10 years old, she becomes sexually receptive and starts tagging along with parties of males who may mate with her. Since she cannot get pregnant at this age, there is no risk of inbreeding; but as she gets older, some instinct tells her to find a new home.

This is a risky time for a female. She must leave the community she was born into and move into another. The females who are already there don't like it, although they have all done the same thing themselves. Luckily the males welcome her, and she does her best to encourage them by mating with as many as possible. But still she does not get pregnant.

▼ *From the age of about six months a young chimp hitches a ride on its mother's back.*

▲ *A female chimpanzee who has moved into another community may not be made welcome at first. Mutual grooming is a sign that the other females have accepted her.*

Eventually, when she is about 14 years old, she is able to have a baby. By this time she has claimed a small "core territory" of her own, which usually provides enough food for her and her baby. Gradually she makes friends among the other females, who gather in nursery groups for companionship and to provide protection against invaders. She has now become part of her adopted community.

Social climbing

A newly arrived female has the lowest possible status in the chimp community. All the other females give her a hard time, and she has to live in the parts of the range that nobody else wants. Gradually, though, she starts to claw her way up. The arrival of even younger females helps, since she can gang up with the other chimps against the newcomers. And since the new girls are now at the bottom of the pecking order, her status rises.

With time she is able to claim a better feeding territory. The other females compete to groom her and act as her childminders. Even when she is quite old and past childbearing, she is still treated with respect.

Built for the job

A full-grown male chimpanzee has the arm strength of three average men, and he is not afraid to use it. Despite this, he usually weighs only about 110 pounds (50kg), so he is light enough to feed in the trees without breaking the branches. Females are even lighter, at about 66 pounds (30kg). Over time chimps' bodies have become specially adapted for climbing, something they can do with ease.

They have extralong fingers and toes for hooking around branches, and long arms for reaching across big gaps. Chimps' eyes face forward to give them stereo vision, so they can see in 3-D like us. This is usually a feature of hunting animals, but in chimps it is more important for judging distances between branches. They also have good color vision for picking out the glow of ripe fruit among the leaves of trees.

Their teeth are adapted for eating a wide range of foods, like ours, but they are a little bigger for chewing leaves and fruit. The males, in particular, have extra-long canine teeth that they use when fighting—and those teeth can be lethal.

◄ *An adult chimp has a black face, but in young animals it is usually pink.*

▲ *With hands and feet that can grip with ease, chimps are expert climbers.*

Knuckle walking

Small monkeys get around in the trees by running over branches, but a chimpanzee is too big for that. Instead, it swings below the branches, and its extralong arms give it a long "stride" so it can move as fast as possible.

It can walk upright, but usually supports its weight on the knuckles of its folded fingers. The skin on its knuckles becomes very thick and tough.

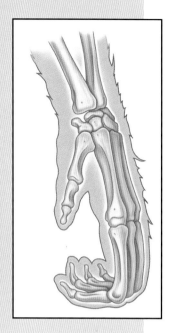

▲ *Chimps usually walk on their knuckles.*

▼ *A chimp has fingernails that are like ours.*

Fingers and thumbs

A chimpanzee's hand is very like a human hand, with sensitive fingertips and nails instead of sharp claws. Most importantly, it can pinch its thumb and fingers together to grip things. Its fingers are much longer than ours, so it cannot bring the tips of its fingers and thumb together for a real precision grip, but it can be surprisingly skillful with small tools.

Scientists think the ability to hold tools was the main reason why chimps became so intelligent—it created the opportunity to develop the intelligence to use them.

Close relations

Chimpanzees are apes, part of a large group of mammals called the primates. The primates include all the apes and monkeys, plus lemurs, tarsiers, lorises, and bushbabies. This group also includes ourselves—because we, too, are just modified apes.

▲ *Orangutans spend most of their lives in trees. Unlike chimps, they are never found in large communities.*

We are the chimps' ~~WRONG~~※ closest relatives, along with the other apes: the gibbons, orangutan, and gorilla. The gibbons are the real acrobats of the ape world. Smaller and lighter than chimps, they have even longer, stronger arms and hurl themselves through the trees with amazing agility and speed. They live in the forests of parts of Southeast Asia, and like chimps they mainly eat ripe fruit.

22 ※ God made all animals they did not evolve / my Proof is the Bible!

Their closest relatives

All the information controlling the development, growth, and maintenance of animals and plants is held in DNA, a complicated molecule found within all living cells. Chimps and humans are different because we have different DNA.

Scientists can now measure the differences between the DNA of various animals. A chimpanzee's DNA is very like that of a gorilla, but it is even more like that of a human. Over 98 percent of our genes are exactly the same.

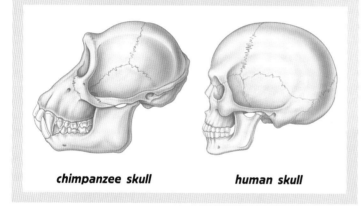

chimpanzee skull   **human skull**

The orangutan is much heavier and moves more slowly, but it still spends most of its time in the trees. It hangs from all four limbs, so it seems to have four arms. Now very scarce, it lives only on the rain forest islands of Sumatra and Borneo.

The giant of the ape world is the gorilla. A big male can weigh up to 400 pounds (180kg), which is far too heavy for most branches to bear. The lighter females and young sometimes feed in the trees like chimps, but gorillas spend most of their time eating leaves on the ground. They live in the rain forests of Central Africa, and like the orangutan they are now very rare.

▼ *The bonobo, or pygmy chimpanzee, has a distinctive hairstyle. Like its bigger relation it lives in Africa.*

Bonobo

There are two types of chimps: the chimpanzee and the bonobo. Bonobos live in the forests south of the Congo River, while chimpanzees live to the north. Bonobos are more lightly built and graceful than chimpanzees, with long, neatly parted black hair on their heads. They also have a different way of life, with communities based on related females rather than males. Their teeth are almost identical to those of our oldest known ancestors.

Intelligence

Most animals spend much of their lives doing things guided by a set of instructions called instincts. Although many animals can learn to change their instinctive behavior with experience, chimps are capable of learning and passing on behavior that is completely noninstinctive.

► *A chimpanzee "fishing" for termites.*

Fishing for termites

Termites make tasty, protein-rich snacks for chimpanzees; but since termites live in fortified nests of sun-baked earth, they can be difficult to get at. A chimpanzee solves the problem by making a "fishing rod" from a slender stick or stem. It slips the rod into a nest entrance and wriggles it so the termites attack, clamping their jaws into it. The chimp then carefully pulls out the rod, complete with termites, and eats them.

Chimpanzees have instincts, too, but a lot of their behavior is guided by what they learn, rather than the instincts they inherit. In some ways this makes life hard, because every chimp has to learn a lot to survive. But it also means they can find new ways of solving old problems and even answers to new problems. Intelligence makes them adaptable.

One way they show this is by using tools. Chimps use stone hammers for cracking nuts, selecting them carefully to suit the job. Since stones are scarce in the rain forest, they look after them carefully and even carry them around. They also make tools, such as leaf sponges for soaking up water and probes for catching burrowing insects. If a tool is not quite right, a chimp will adjust it or make another. It is always thinking ahead.

▶ *Chimps show their intelligence in some astonishing ways. Like most wild animals they pick up parasites that give them stomach troubles, but they deal with this by eating a medicinal plant that works like an antibiotic. They make a point of looking for the plants and carefully selecting the parts they want. Then they swallow the dry, bristly leaves without chewing, as we would swallow a doctor's pill.*

Forest ape

A chimpanzee is basically a creature of the tropical forest. It lives mainly on fruit and is adapted for climbing trees to get it. Chimps also sleep in trees, making fresh leafy nests every night.

D espite this, chimps can make a living in a wide variety of habitats. We always imagine them in the dense, steamy rain forest, but they can also live in dry woodland or even open grasslands where trees are found only in river valleys. They sometimes move from one type of habitat to another to find food and may even prefer the variety.

In the rain forest trees bear fruit at any time. There is always

▲ *A chimp settles down for the night in its nest of twigs and leaves.*

Shrinking habitats

A century ago chimpanzees lived all over the tropical green belt of Central and West Africa in an area almost as big as the United States. The whole region was a patchwork of evergreen rain forests, open woodland, and savanna grassland. The chimps lived wherever they found fruiting trees, and there were millions of them.

Today most of this landscape has been destroyed. The forests are being felled for their valuable timber, and the land turned into fields. The chimps have retreated to the few areas of wilderness that still remain. Most live in the rain forests around the Congo River, but they also survive in parts of West Africa. They are becoming rarer all the time.

fruit somewhere; but since there is no real pattern, it can be difficult to find. In the drier woodlands, by contrast, all the trees tend to come into fruit at about the same time. It's a feast, and the chimps make the most of it. When the fruiting season is over, though, they are better off in the rain forest.

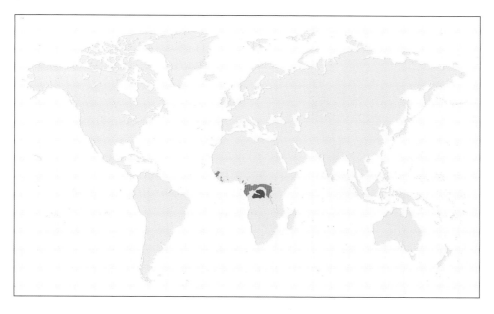

▲ *Chimpanzees can live in a wide variety of habitats. This one is in a coastal mangrove.*

◀ *Map showing areas of the world where chimpanzees (shown in red) and bonobos (purple) live.*

Chimps and us

In Central Africa some people eat chimpanzees. They kill the adults with shotguns and sell them in the local markets as "bushmeat." The orphaned babies are captured alive and sold to illegal animal traders for a few dollars. The traders pack them in crates and ship them all over the world. Most of them do not reach their destinations; they die on the way.

◀ *Orphaned chimps being cared for in a sanctuary.*

Some of the survivors end up in research laboratories, where they are used for research into human diseases like AIDS. Others are sold as pets, and they are often abandoned when they grow too big. A few find fame as film or TV stars. The lucky ones finish up in zoos and sanctuaries, and some are returned to Africa, where they are released in protected areas of forest. There they can try to live as their parents did before they were aware that people existed.

It seems odd that our closest relatives are treated so badly. It is particularly sad because there are probably fewer than 200,000 chimpanzees remaining in the wild. If we do not start giving them the respect they deserve, they could soon disappear altogether.

Chimp rescue

A few people have made it their business to rescue orphaned chimpanzees and give them good homes with other chimps. There are chimpanzee sanctuaries all over the world and several in tropical Africa.

The chimpanzees are found in airport luggage, nightclubs, and run-down zoos or dressed up as photographers' dummies. They often know how to do tricks but have no idea how to find food. Their rescuers have to teach them by example, by climbing trees and eating leaves and fruit. But they cannot teach them how to survive the dangerous world beyond the boundary fence, so these chimps will never know what it means to be truly wild and free.

▲ *Chimps were popular circus attractions for many years.*

▼ *Deprived of their mothers' milk, these orphan chimps thrive on a bottled substitute.*

Further reading

Amazing Monkeys
by Robert Hynes (National Geographic Society, 1999).

Apes, Language, and the Human Mind
by Sue Savage-Rumbaugh, Stuart Shanker, and Talbot Taylor (OUP, 1998).

The Great Apes
by Jennifer Lindsey and Jane Goodall (Metro Books, 1999).

I Didn't Know That Chimps Use Tools
by Claire Llewellyn, Chris Shields, and Jo Moore (Copper Beech Books, 1999).

In the Shadow of Man
by Jane Goodall, Hugo van Lawick, and Stephen Jay Gould (Houghton Mifflin, 1998).

Jane Goodall—40 Years at Gombe
by Jennifer Lindsey, Dr. Jane Goodall, and Gilbert Grosvenor (Stewart Tabori and Chang, 2000).

My Life with the Chimpanzees
by Jane Goodall (Minstrel Books, 2000).

Primates: Apes, Monkeys, Prosimians
by Thane Maynard (Cincinnati Zoo, 1997) .

Web Sites
www.chimps.org
www.fortunecity.com
www.geocities.com
www.savethechimps.org

Useful Addresses
The Bonobo Protection Fund
Georgia State University, Georgia State University Plaza, Atlanta, Georgia 3030.

The Jane Goodall Institute (Canada)
PO Box 477, Victoria Station, Westmount, Quebec H3Z 2Y6, Canada.

The Jane Goodall Institute (U.S.)
PO Box 14890, Silver Springs, MD 20911-4890.

Worldwide Fund for Nature
1250 24th Street NW, Washington DC 20037.

Glossary

ancestors: animals from which chimps have developed over many, many generations.

canine teeth: four pointed teeth between the incisors and the molars.

core territory: area a female chimp relies on to provide enough food for her and her offspring.

DNA: chemical responsible for passing hereditary characters from parents to offspring.

gene: basic unit of heredity. Part of a DNA molecule that passes on a code for a given trait, for example, hair color, eye color, or size.

habitat: the kind of place where a particular animal lives.

heredity: passing of characteristics from one generation to the next.

hierarchy: existence of ranks in a community of animals, with some individuals dominating others.

inbreeding: breeding between closely related animals.

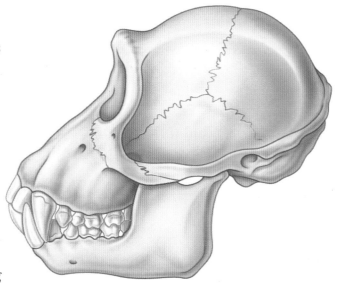

instinctive behavior: ability an animal is born with to respond to different situations in standard ways.

mammal: kind of animal that is warm-blooded and has a backbone. Most are covered with fur. Females have glands that produce milk to feed their young.

parasite: animal that lives on or in another animal from which it gets nourishment.

primate: one of a group of mammals in the order Anthropoidea, including the apes, monkeys, and humans.

tropical: having to do with or found in the tropics.

Index